TEN HOUSES

Edited by Oscar Riera Ojeda

Eduardo Souto Moura

Rockport Publishers, Inc.
Gloucester, Massachusetts

First published in the United States of America by

Rockport Publishers, Inc.

33 Commercial Street

Gloucester, Massachusetts 01930

Telephone: 508-282-9590

Fax: 508-283-2742

Distributed to the book trade and art trade in the United States of America by

North Light Books, an imprint of

F & W Publications

1504 Dana Avenue

Cincinnati, Ohio 45207

Telephone: 513-531-2222

Other distribution by

Rockport Publishers, Inc.

Gloucester, Massachusetts 01930

ISBN 1-56496-394-2

10 9 8 7 6 5 4 3 2 1

Cover photo: Miramar House. Photo by Luís Ferreira Alves.

Back cover images are of projects on pages (from left, top to bottom) 14, 22, 32, 40, 52, 62, 72, 84, 90, 100.

Printed in Hong Kong.

Graphic design: Lucas H. Guerra / Oscar Riera Ojeda

Layout: Oscar Riera Ojeda

Contents

Foreword

by Oscar Riera Ojeda

In the early eighties when I began to study architecture, I devoured every pertinent book or publication that came my way (although in those days the number of publications was more limited than today). I remember that my first exposure to Portuguese culture occurred as I flipped through possibly the last magazine in the library, an edition of the Japanese publication *A+U* from the 1970s, which featured the work of Alvaro Siza (Souto Moura's mentor, with whom he worked during his first professional years). After looking at thousands of pages displaying, almost exclusively, Postmodern architecture, my curiosity was awakened by this poetic Mediterranean architecture, an architecture that did not seem to be an isolated product, nor alien to its context. It is in the environment of this Portuguese reality that Souto Moura designed the ten houses compiled here.

Several years passed and while the rest of the world continued to theorize about and construct Postmodern architecture, the few published works from Portugal (except for the inexplicable buildings of Tomas Taveira) focused on a school of thought that remained faithful to the Modern spirit. During these years, to swim against the current seemed to be the natural but solitary path for this small nation.

It took several years for the critics to discover the value of this constant route, but when its achievements were recognized and given the hierarchical label of "regionalist," the maturity, clarity, profundity, and resolution of ideas of Portuguese architecture greatly surpassed the restrictions this name wished to impose upon it. Perhaps the people most surprised by this change in attitude were the Portuguese architects themselves, who, without greatly modifying their posture and without abandoning their culture for two decades, went from an unrecognized entity to the center of the international architectural debate as a source of permanent reference. Portuguese architects do only what they have to do, where and when it must be done. This sparks our interest and describes their rudimentary practice, which in its simplicity brings architecture to its just cause. Souto Moura explained the challenge of building the Casa Das Artes Cultural Center in Oporto by stating, "Omitting was more important than proposing, filling and shaving were more important than designing, and simplicity was more important than composition." For the Sports Area Cafe in Braga, he "saw a wall, near the water."

Vilarinha Garden Pavilion, Porto, Portugal

The work of Eduardo Souto Moura first came to my attention with the appearance of a small monograph published in 1990 by the Catalan publisher Gustavo Gili. Its cover included a photographic detail (reproduced here) of the Annexes in the Rua de Vilarinha in Porto. I remember the impact that this image had on me, because in it I saw the very synthesis of architecture. The connection of the building with its surroundings, the presence of history, the rigorous and coherent pursuit of new interpretations for each everyday problem—all were apparent in this detail where technique and poetry achieve equilibrium. The materials are well known, but their juxtaposition and the way they are used are not.

The intellectual resolution of detail in the work of Eduardo Souto Moura acquires a degree of Mies-like obsession; a rich variety of materials is integrated beautifully with the elegant and pure simplicity that reigns in these houses. The intelligent way materials come together in a detail speaks about the pursuit of transition and autonomy. It contributes to a more dynamic play of the composition of planes, at times solid, at times light.

To speak of these ten houses based on their details can be compared to entering a house through the service door or leafing backwards through a book; however, this is not the option chosen by most of us. Souto Moura does not design his houses merely through their details, but in them he reflects the order and the essence that enhance the clarity of his architecture.

Nevogilde House II, Oporto, Portugal

Alcanena House, Torres Novas, Portugal

Miramar House, Vila Nova de Gaia, Portugal

Boavista Avenue House, Porto, Portugal

Bom Jesus House, Braga, Portugal

Bom Jesus House, Braga, Portugal

Bom Jesus House, Braga, Portugal

Baião House, Baião, Portugal

Maia House, Maia, Portugal

Maia House, Maia, Portugal

Maia House, Maia, Portugal

Tavira House, Algarve, Portugal

Introduction

The Visibility of the Invisible
by José Paulo dos Santos

The discovery of a pattern seems to be inherent in the human activity of making. What are the criteria that make certain models, as opposed to others, worthy of being copied?

In a country such as Portugal, which is profoundly aware of its roots and traditions, the act of dwelling, permeated by a strong sense of the certainty of function, has remained unaltered through time.

Deeply ingrained habits of inhabitation, and a strong sense of intimacy and use make the range of options available to us clear, if not definitive.

The house becomes the disguise for spaces that vary according to function and use.

My understanding of Eduardo Souto Moura's architecture is an extension of the immediate understanding and evaluation I make of the local conditions and constraints and of all constraints in general.

To date, a significant part of his commissions have been devoted to the design of single-family houses for—within the context of the country—particularly privileged clients.

Contrary to first assumptions, Souto Moura has never—in the past two decades— designed the same house twice.

He sees the house as an object with a precise program: with fixed denominators —living, services, bedrooms, and intermediate zones—and distribution vestibule and corridors that serve as adjustable spaces.

The program is thus almost invariable in the resolution of its parts. Each house has an established framework of predictable hierarchies.

He always keeps his eyes open to possibilities, even if his mind is rooted in the rational and his soul is rooted in local tradition.

Contradiction and ambiguity are always present in Souto Moura's work. The focal point is the process of production rather than the product itself.

o design a house—or simply to design—is thus an act of intelligence. It is also an act of seduction.

There is, on one hand, the unseen revealed by the pencil, and on the other, local conditions and all that the architect can lure the client into accepting.

Souto Moura always thinks of his projects at length in order to produce short statements; he considers each of his projects in depth, so that the result is felt through the "minimal" expression of the work. He always establishes a precarious equilibrium between intelligence and seduction; between what is always present by not being evocative and what is sensed through its materiality; between the parti and the object.

Acts of intelligence need no announcement—their ominous presence is felt by not being seen. While acts of seduction, to be seen, require good bait.

The houses of Souto Moura are not scenic, as Mies van der Rohe's houses are. Despite the apparent similarity, with vertical planes or columns always supporting slabs, the content is quite strictly controlled in the traditional sense. Free-floating space is avoided. With transparency always apparent, the intimate nature of space and objects prevail. In this sense, Souto Moura's work never expresses the phenomenon, but rather the intimate essence of the phenomenon. It seems that, as Hugo Haring noted, form is the result of the "intrinsic dwelling within the object."

According to Souto Moura, all houses are simultaneously similar yet different because the site so deserves). As Aldo Rossi (a reference for Souto Moura) has said, "with the architect never being carried away by people or things, which he considers useless, progress in art and science is dependent on continuity and firmness, the only variables that allow for change."

The point of interest of Souto Moura's houses is not their individual qualities or description, but a re-analysis of how the same program is presented, worked, adjusted in order to be addressed to the mind and eye.

Souto Moura never places a volume anywhere at random. For him, the house

Apartment Renovation, Braga, Portugal

either through its absence enhances the place—a ruin within the countryside—or through its massing, reorders the site—an omnipresent wall that slides into a canopy. The house never sits in the landscape; it belongs to it.

The building of a house purports to be truthful to construction, even if it has to rely on alibis to resolve localized details, because elements of construction cannot always be faithful to the architectural concept.

If truth is not always fully achievable, adjustments make it almost consistent, for as Vieira de Campos has written, "artifice plays with an expectancy of truth, being used to meet with an idea of architecture."

This page and next, Nevogilde Apartment, Porto, Portugal

The wall and the slab carry most of the load in the plastic resolution of parts.

Traditional elements of the interior—skirting, frames—are reduced to their dematerialized opposites—to nonbeing. Plasticity requires formal continuity.

Materials such as stone, wood, concrete, and glass suggest that for Souto Moura, using Ian G. McEwen's words, "the ordering of the dance is a reflection of their adornment. As kosmos clothes the body to make it appear, so, through dance, kosmos clothes the ground to make it appear like the radiance of the moon."

For Souto Moura, the house is perceived as—in Ian G. McEwen's words—"the skin that is the Homeric word for living body, which was understood as a surface and the bearer of visibility, visibility being the guarantor of existence or being. For the Greek appearing was surface. . . For them, when a woman adorned herself, she wrapped her skin in a second skin or body, in order to bring the living surface so clothed to light; to make it appear. If women in ancient Greece were essentially invisible, the cosmetic made them visible."

Built architecture embodies tensions between a concept and the ability to convey it to clients.

Detailing becomes the silent witness of this struggle. Or the second skin or body. Or maybe God.

Porto, July 1997

Nevogilde House I
Oporto, Portugal

I n this rectangular plot, the boundaries were defined by party walls. A longitudinal wall crosses the building, separating the annex and service areas from the house itself. The structure is enclosed on the sides and open at the ends, with the bedrooms facing east and the living room opening onto a garden facing west.

A square central courtyard organizes the circulation.

The house is designed to the limits of its site, and its equilibrium is precarious.

Were it not for the stone walls and the neighboring house, it would seem that nothing had yet been planned.

Above: Addressing the contrasting nature of traditional and modern elements, an iron gate slides behind the stone wall, allowing entry to the garage and service areas.

Opposite Page: Designed for year-round use, this rectilinear house is masked from the street by a rough-hewn granite wall that echoes the horizontality of the residence. Traditional means of cutting and mounting the stones indicate strong references and respect for local typologies in this coastal town.

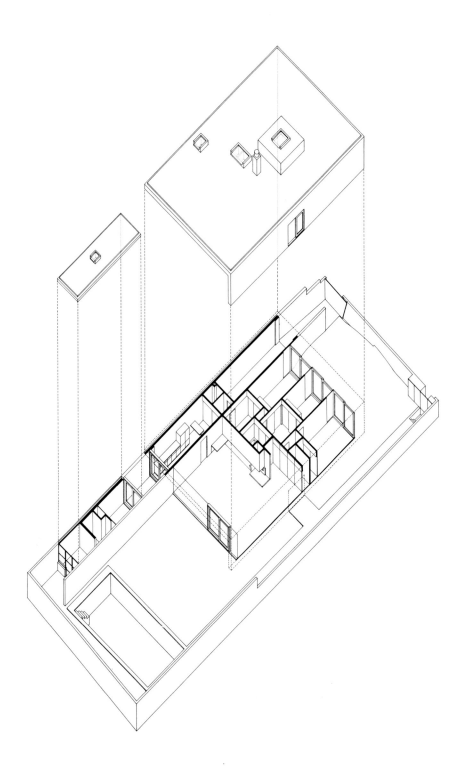

This Page: Recessed to ensure protection from summer sunlight, the three bedrooms are defined by a curtain wall running parallel to the outer granite wall. The bedrooms overlook a small courtyard that is partitioned from the garage by an extension of a wall jutting out from the interior.

Opposite Page: After crossing a small iron gate similar to the one by the garage, a pathway leads to the main entrance of the house, located by a palm tree, and to the swimming pool at the end of the lot.

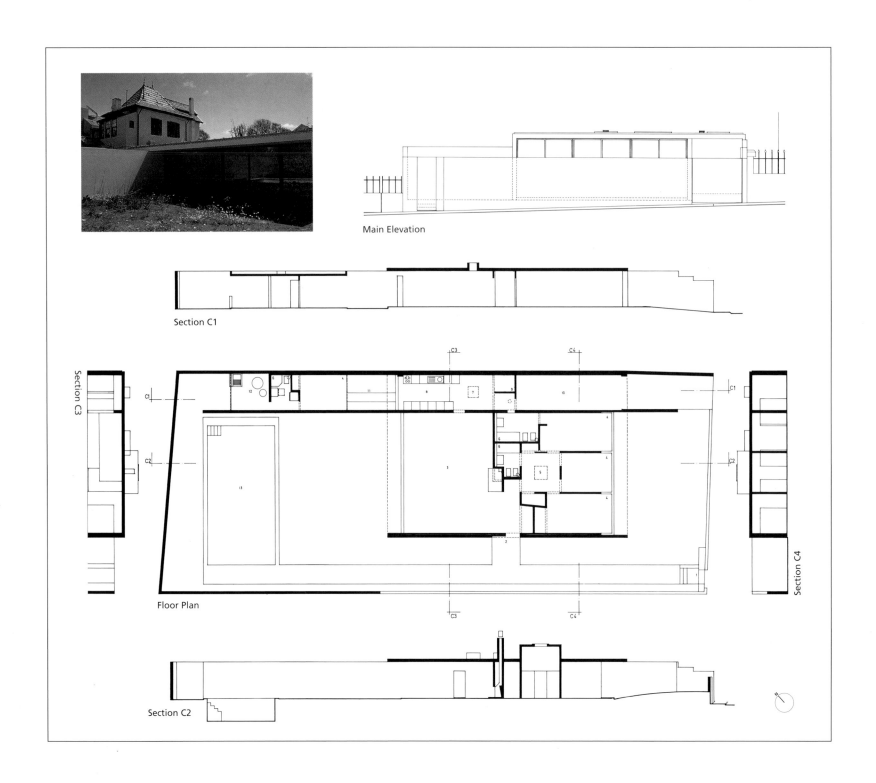

Main Elevation

Section C1

Section C3

Section C4

Floor Plan

Section C2

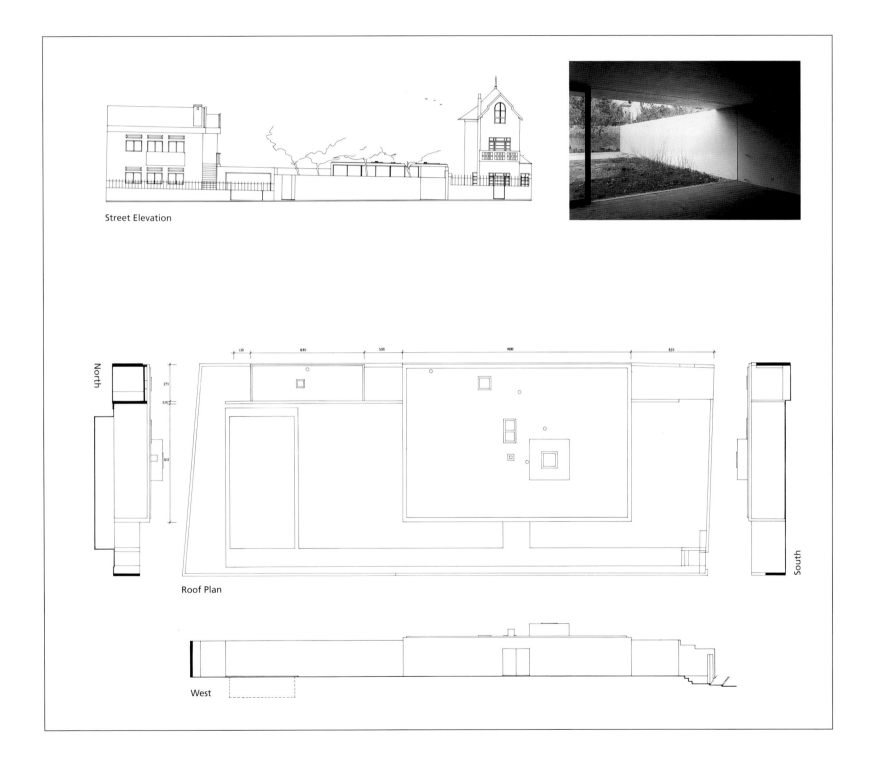

Street Elevation

North

273

0.15

9.12

130   8.60   3.00   18.00   6.50

Roof Plan

South

West

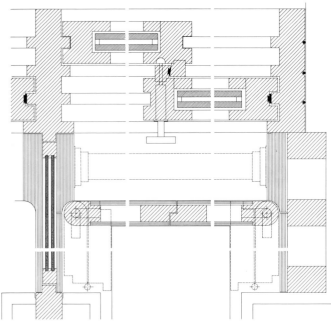

Horizontal Section Through Bedroom Window

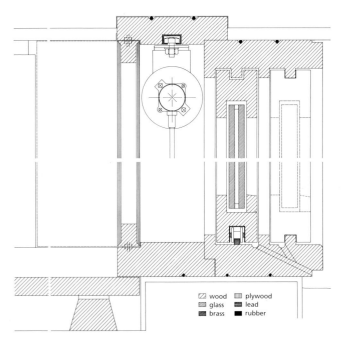

▨ wood	▥ plywood
▨ glass	▦ lead
■ brass	■ rubber

Vertical Section Through Bedroom Window

This Page: *The bedrooms (top and center) are marked by the dissolution of interior and exterior boundaries. Windows form a seamless unit with ceiling, floor, and interior walls, and can be covered with movable screens for greater privacy.*

Left and Opposite Page: *A cubic and modular hall connects bed, bath, and storage areas. The mirrored panel and square skylight open the space and reflect their surrounding interior geometries.*

Nevogilde House II
Oporto, Portugal

The site is made up of a set of separately acquired lots. Dislocating walls, moving the earth, choosing the stones—this was essentially the virtual making of the house. With a large and complex program, the house sits parallel to the existing site wall. The program is spread along a service gallery, the backbone of the building.

The various parts of the house can be identified from the south by openings that access the lawn. On the north side, only the door indicates the entrance.

From the street, there is only a gate, opening the place for us.

Above: *Entry along a path reveals a series of granite columns rising in the distance atop a low-lying wall, recalling ancient structures. Recessed from view by a tennis court and surrounding flora and trees, the site appears to be an untouched extension of the landscape.*

Opposite Page: *The columns, in unison with the house and its surrounding vegetation, allude to ruins and anticipate the gridlike sequence of rooms and fenestration.*

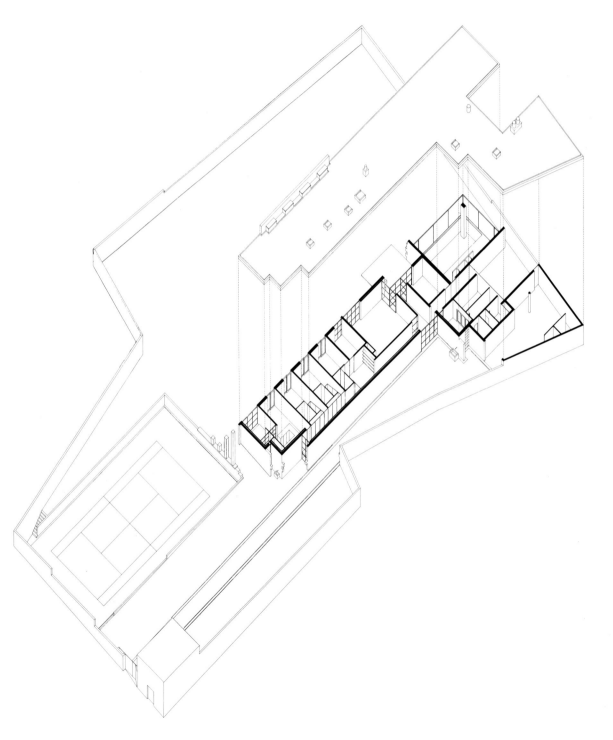

Left: *The main entrance is sheltered by a glass canopy.*

Opposite Page: *At the end of the patio, a large gate encloses an open garage. Granite fountains, situated along the property to collect rainwater, double as sculptural forms.*

This Page: *Extending from the tennis court to the main access, a path opens onto an entry courtyard lined with native shrubs and flowering plants. Built with local stone, the courtyard mediates between the domains of the site and the surrounding terrain.*

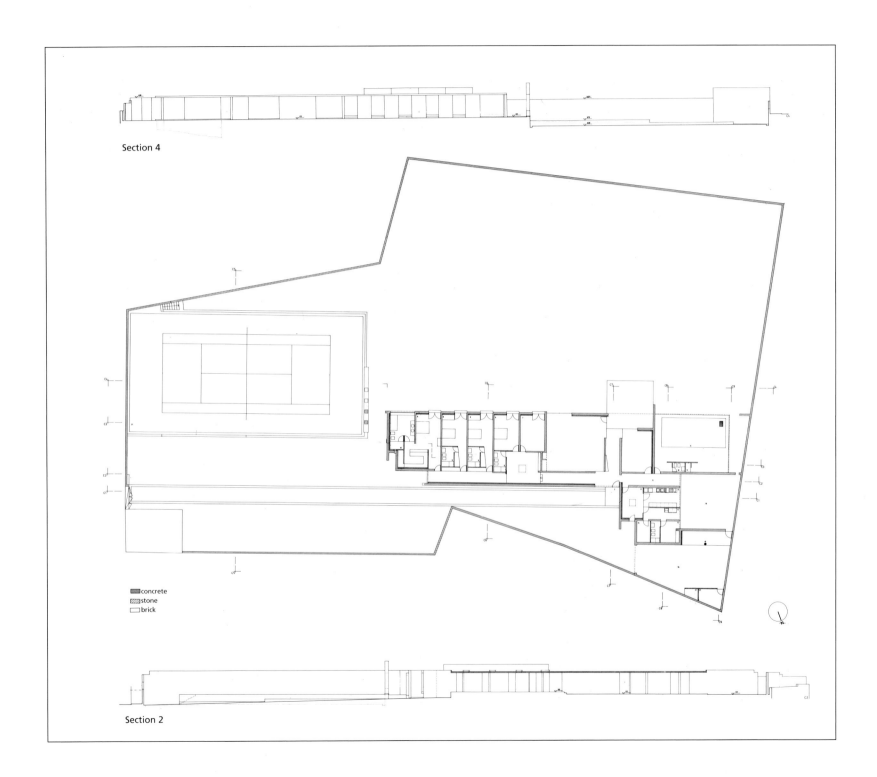

Section 4

concrete
stone
brick

Section 2

Master Bathroom

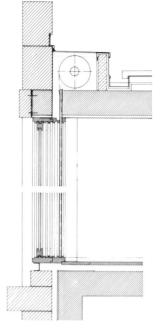

Bedroom

Indoor Swimming Pool

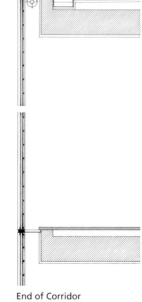

End of Corridor

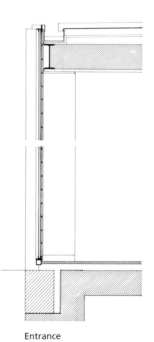

Entrance

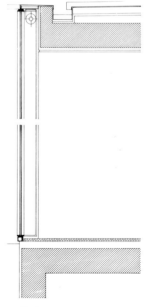

Kitchen

This Page: With marble sinks, walls, and flooring, the master bath is a study of reflected space. Stainless-steel-framed mirrored doors give access to the room and its shower compartment while expanding the interior. The indoor swimming pool is surrounded by curtain walls that eliminate spatial boundaries.

Opposite Page: In a finely articulated contrast of materials, a brass division connects the granite wall and wooden bedroom door. Corridors reveal the interaction of opaqued glass doors with brick and stone walls.

Algarve House

Algarve, Portugal

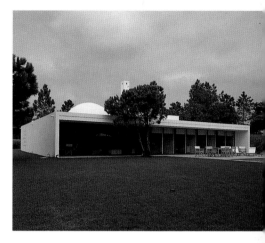

The project is a vacation house located in Algarve, on a housing estate next to a golf course. Local building regulations strongly limited the project: the house should be white, with one floor alone occupying only twenty percent of the site, with no annexes.

Due to the client's program, as well as existing regulations, the scheme for the house appears as a parallelepiped volume standing on the edge of the golf course.

Typologically, the house can be considered a cross between a certain southern vernacular architecture (with strong Arabic influences) and, strange as it may seem, some Chinese houses (the project was partially designed in Macau).

For good or bad we always redraw our past—and in this case past built works were taken into account. Some images by Le Corbusier were used to resolve detailing problems. Models and references confirm and revise the initial proposal, then become images to pursue. It is as if things know when they have to happen.

Above: Seemingly an enclosed structure, an open back elevation looks upon the swimming pool and the golf course green. The recessed window frame conceals bedrooms and living rooms.

Opposite Page: Placed on the edge of a golf course, the house, a clearly defined white box with highly articulated geometric volumes on its roof, appears in distinct contrast with its surrounding context. An image almost surreal in composition, and drawing on Medieval notions of a perfect, walled city, the parallelepiped is contained by a concrete shell. Its continuity is disrupted on the left side by the entrance door and punctuated on the right by cubic voids screening a service patio.

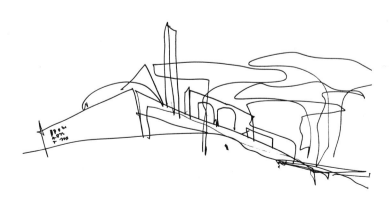

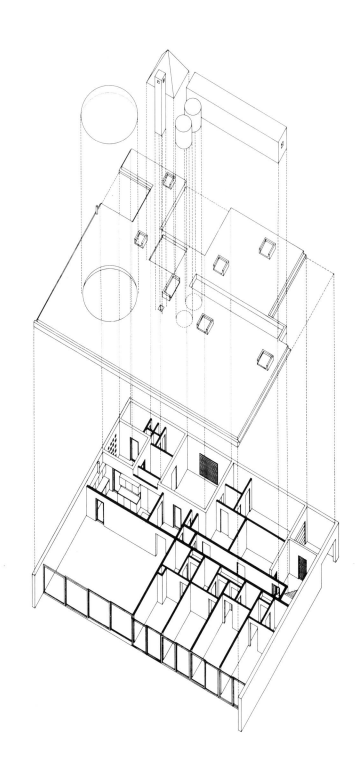

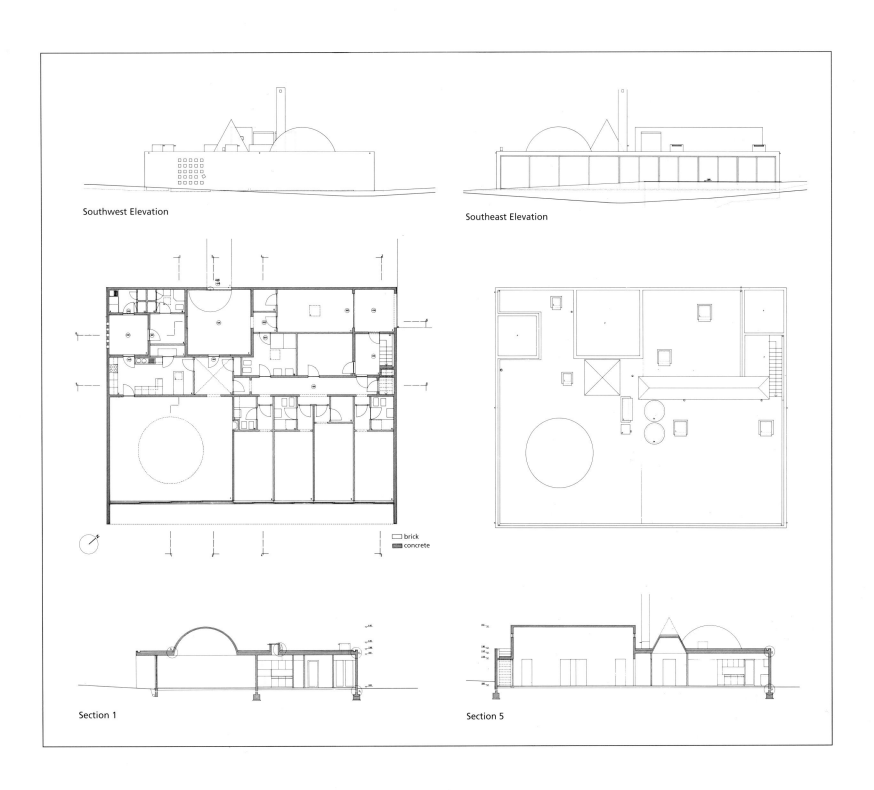

Southwest Elevation

Southeast Elevation

brick
concrete

Section 1

Section 5

Right: *Three living room views. This space is framed by terra-cotta floors and double-rail glass panels, which can open to the center or the outside, allowing direct transit onto the golf course. The plaster-finish dome forms a sculptural void within the space.*

Opposite Page: *Terra-cotta flooring is carried through the corridor, where white painted doors assume different hues from the changing light of a small skylight.*

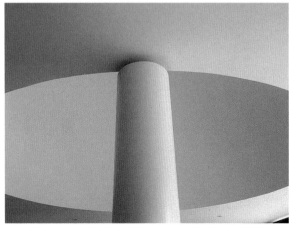

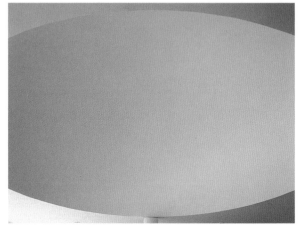

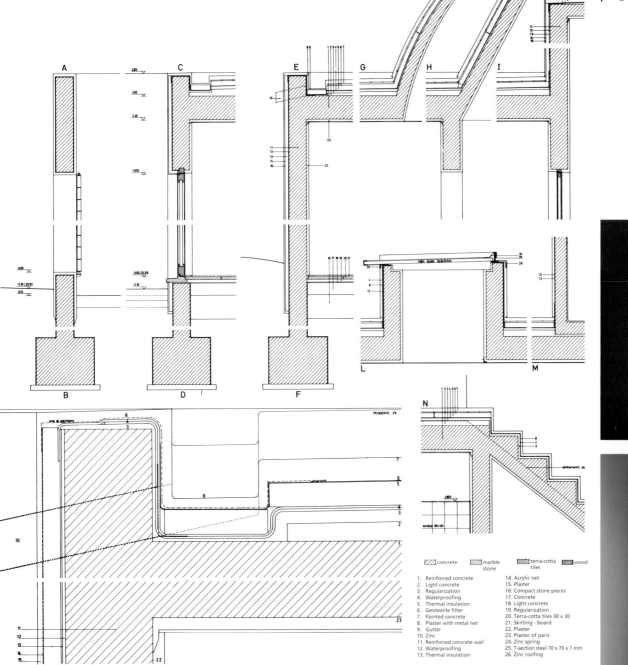

▨ concrete	▨ marble stone	▨ terra-cotta tiles	▨ wood

1. Reinforced concrete
2. Light concrete
3. Regularization
4. Waterproofing
5. Thermal insulation
6. Geotextile filter
7. Painted concrete
8. Plaster with metal net
9. Gutter
10. Zinc
11. Reinforced concrete wall
12. Waterproofing
13. Thermal insulation
14. Acrylic net
15. Plaster
16. Compact stone pieces
17. Concrete
18. Light concrete
19. Regularization
20. Terra-cotta tiles 30 x 30
21. Skirting - board
22. Plaster
23. Plaster of paris
24. Zinc spring
25. T-section steel 70 x 70 x 7 mm
26. Zinc roofing

Alcanena House

Torres Novas, Portugal

The initial sketches for the project resembled a nearby Roman villa. As the project developed, the house gradually lost that visual clue, with only the essential physical elements of the building remaining. The site had been marked with rows of vines—parallel lines cut by a nearly orthogonal system of paths. The house sits almost in the middle of a small hill, in the center of the site.

The house does not look like a single unit, but is spread out in three volumes—bedrooms, living rooms, and service quarters—around a central patio. A U-shaped gallery surrounding the patio links them together.

The project's reference axes (also orthogonal) do not impose themselves on the site's compositional lines. With their foci in the center of the patio, where they turn almost forty-five degrees, they enhance the landscape.

When the work had begun, an unnecessary water tower was demolished, a cellar was dug, and the steel window frames were replaced with natural-colored aluminum ones.

The surrounding landscape is reflected in mirrored glass windows amid white walls of stone and brick.

Above: Viewed from afar, it is a site unseen, a white stone wall lying low against the hill and immersed in the surrounding topography.

Opposite Page: A road flanked by vineyards approaches the house, which is perched atop a gently rising hill. The residence, solitary in character, does not interrupt the continuity of the surrounding plain and sits in quiet harmony with the other, more distant houses of this small town.

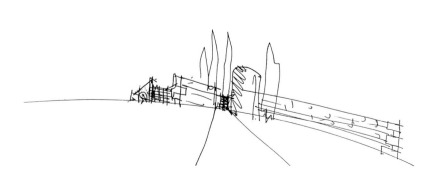

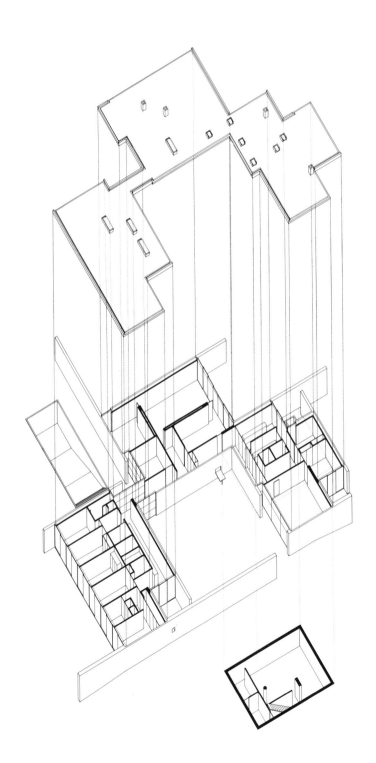

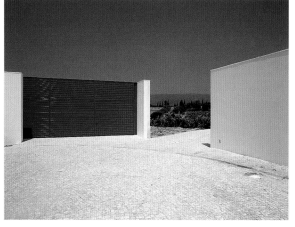

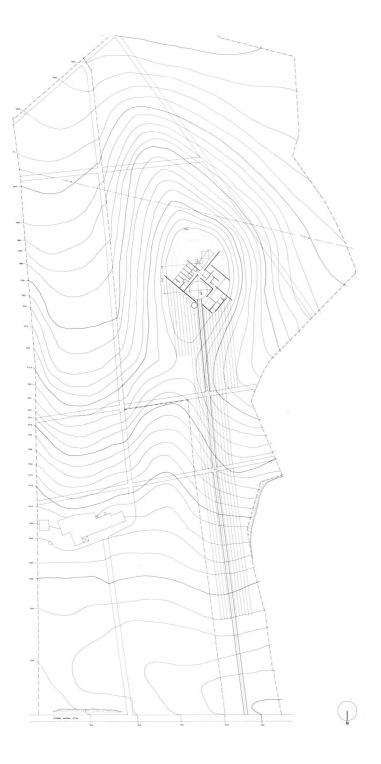

This Page: Acting as a central unit, and sparsely populated with local trees and a rain catchment, the patio allows access to the main and service wings. The center photograph is of the patio facing the end of the corridor, behind the brick wall, where mirrored glass reflects and expands the space.

Opposite Page: The main road affords oblique entry to the central patio. Circular in shape and consisting of small stones, the patio is enclosed by a larger orthogonal frame. The garage is situated to the right of the entry.

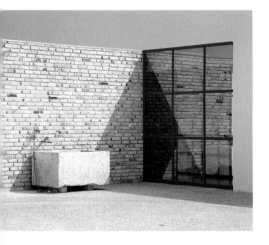

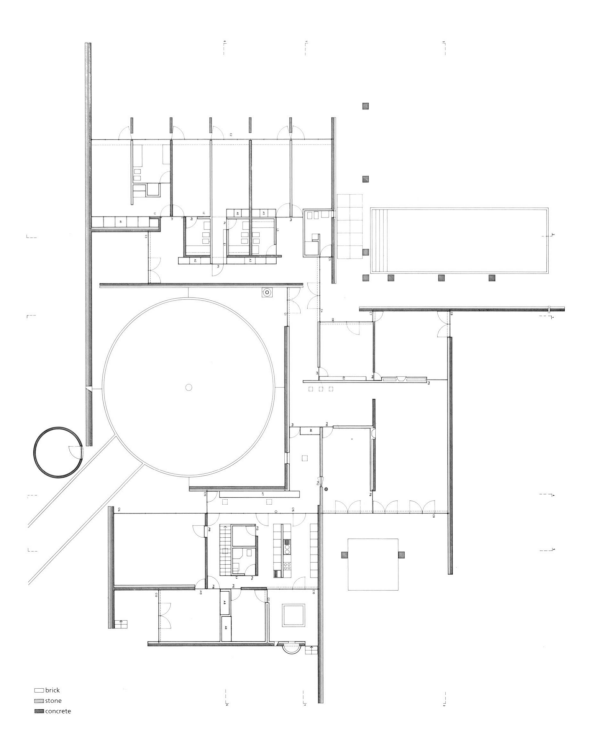

☐ brick
▨ stone
▦ concrete

Left: *With the patio wall brought into the main entry to intersect a floating ceiling panel, interior and exterior walls are in constant motion. The brick and white planes contrast with deep wood flooring, further enhanced by transparent panes of glass.*

Opposite Page: *The contrast of materials is evident at the main entry, where the layered brick of the patio wall accentuates the additional textures of the stone water catchment and the glass entry door.*

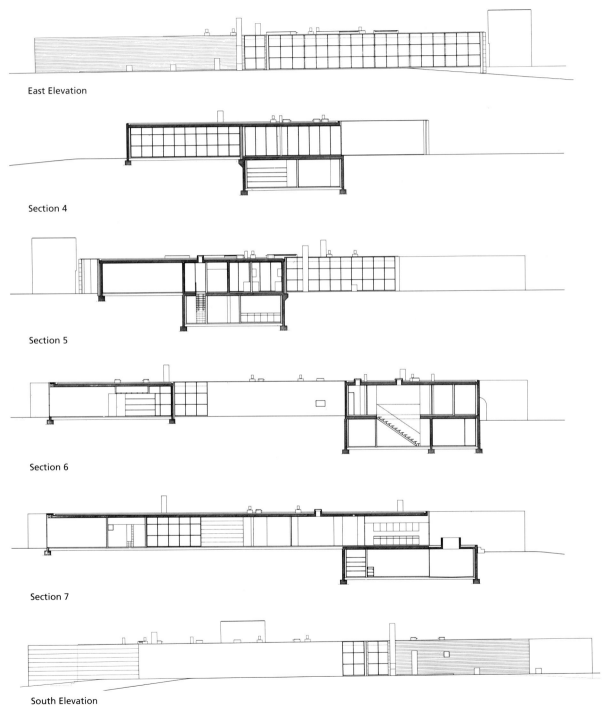

East Elevation

Section 4

Section 5

Section 6

Section 7

South Elevation

Miramar House

Vila Nova de Gaia, Portugal

The site was essentially defined by a group of trees surrounded by granite walls. The granite walls were integrated, where appropriate, into the structure, forming several parts of the house itself—the garage, patios, rooms, and living areas.

A concrete slab above the ground floor serves as the roof and, when doubled over, closes the house at both ends.

On the sides, glass doorways allow one to see outside as far as possible: up to three meters to the road-side wall, between pine trees, and toward the sea that lies beyond the walls.

The project seems simple, and that is what was intended; as the Poet has taught, only "the exact word of any public use."
(Eugénio de Andrade, "Expresso," 5/23/87)

This Page: Trees and lawn act as interstitial space, mediating the dialogue of the plaster and stone walls that define the site.

Opposite Page: A granite wall, adjacent to a yellow volume and a white suspended ceiling, forms a private enclosure allowing entry to the residence.

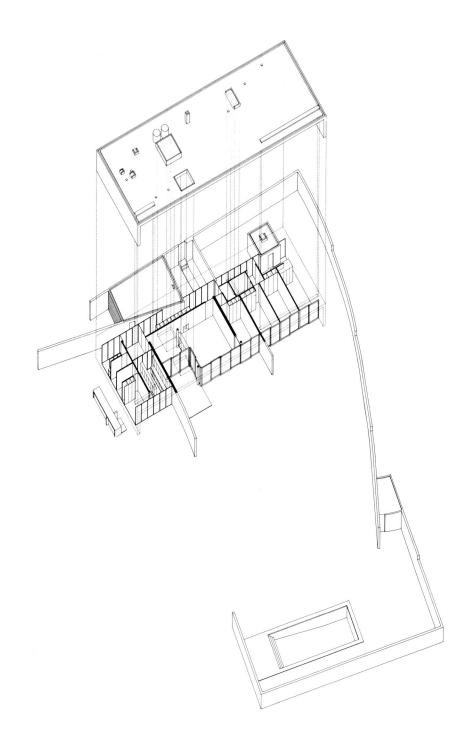

This Page: Bedrooms, walled in glass, bring exterior views into private areas. The notions of interior and exterior space are further transposed in the living room. Timber floors, extended to the outdoor space, are enclosed by a cantilevered roof, glass panels, and a granite wall.

Opposite Page: The recessed entry patio affords views that cut through the house, revealing private and social rooms, and the garden just beyond. A rear detail shows concrete solids and glass voids interacting to provide volumetric definition.

Right: *From the kitchen and service hall, and through the long and narrow corridor, access is given to the private areas—left side of photograph—and the dining and living spaces on the right.*

Opposite Page: *With doors closed, the entry area becomes more static in nature. When open, a fluid connection goes through social and private areas of the house. Mirrored glass doors expand the narrow space, capturing and reflecting the textures of the wood patterned windows.*

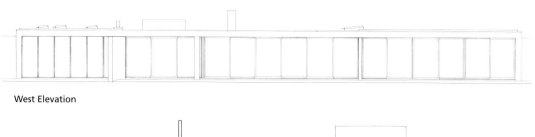

West Elevation

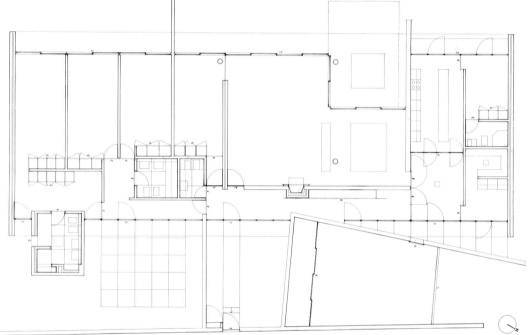

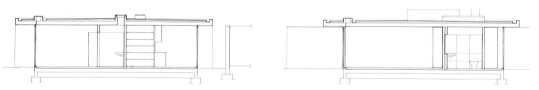

Section 1

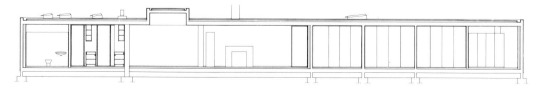

Section 10

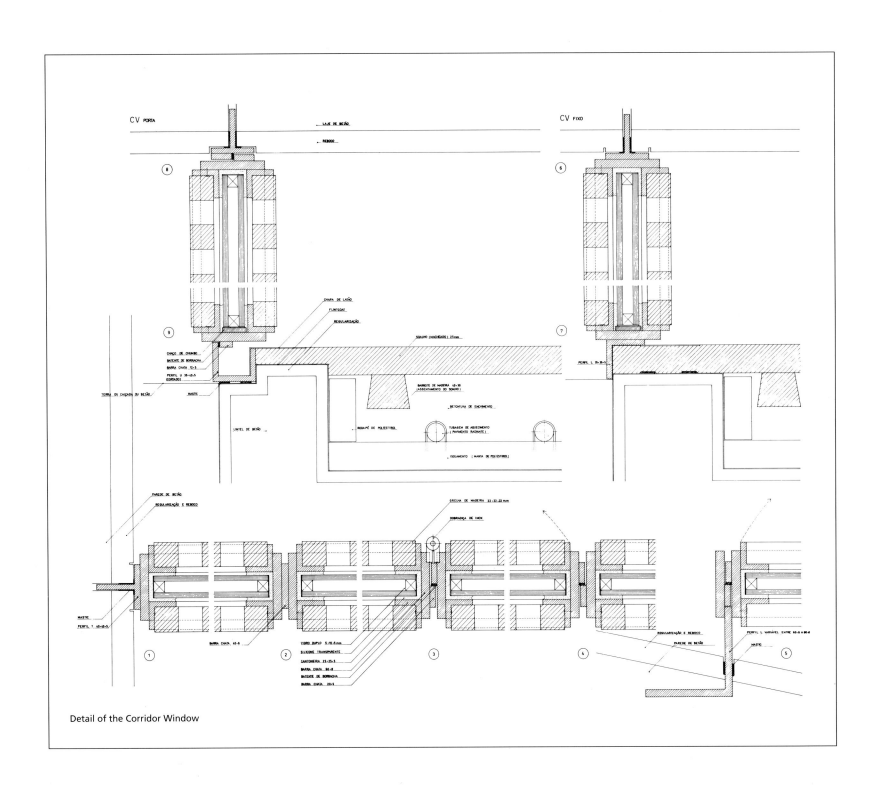

CV PORTA

CV FIXO

Detail of the Corridor Window

Left: Public and private corridors run parallel to the longest side of the rectangular house. From the entry hall, doors to private spaces open to form an enfilade that draws light inside. Textured windows, clad in painted steel framing with wooden overlay, continue the striations of the floor, wrapping and gently enclosing the space.

Boavista Avenue House

Porto, Portugal

T his house is a collage of elements from other houses that I have designed, such as the Casa das Artes, and houses in Alcanena, Vilarinha, and Quinta do Lago. It was built using stones from a convent school and a ruin that was known as the "Sleeping Beauty."

The stones are fake in that they are not load-bearing. Leaning against concrete walls, they become the mineral texture of a painting. The fountain was once part of a window; the stones that make up the veranda and cornices, placed randomly, do not conform to standard masonry practices.

Incidentally, the "Sleeping Beauty" house was originally designed for Alves dos Reis, former director of the Bank of Portugal, who was arrested for forging banknotes.

Above: *The curving path granting approach is encompassed by foliage that further conceals the residence from direct view.*

Opposite Page: *Modest in scale and spartan in character, the house barely rises above a low-lying granite wall. Much of the stonework is taken from stones from the site.*

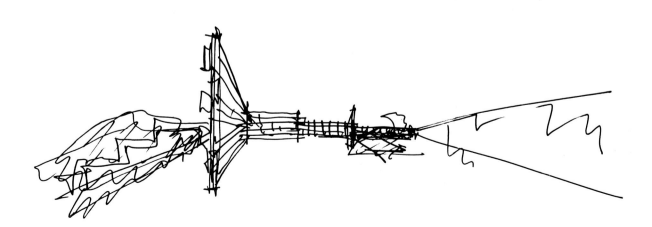

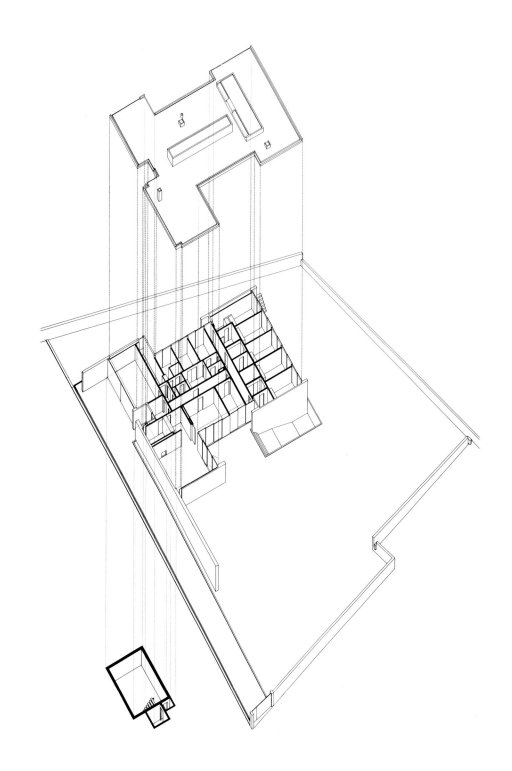

This Page: *From the exterior, living and dining rooms disappear behind intersecting mirrored glass panels. Seen from the interior, the ceiling appears suspended above the continuous, angular curtain wall. Containing shutters within, the windows are free to give multiplaned, panoramic views and unobstructed access to the outdoors.*

Opposite Page: *The outdoor swimming pool, lying next to the bedroom wall, appears as a reflective surface against the surrounding grass. The bedrooms are in linear procession and when their doors are opened, suspended ceilings are revealed.*

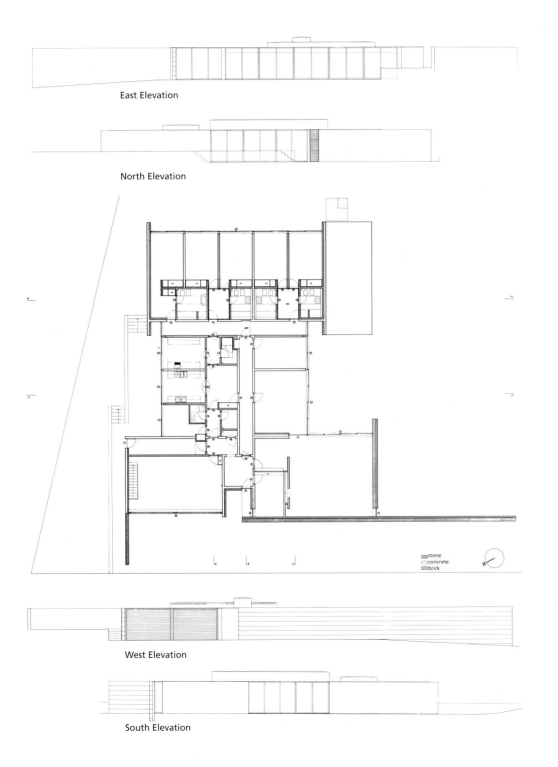

East Elevation

North Elevation

stone
concrete
brick

West Elevation

South Elevation

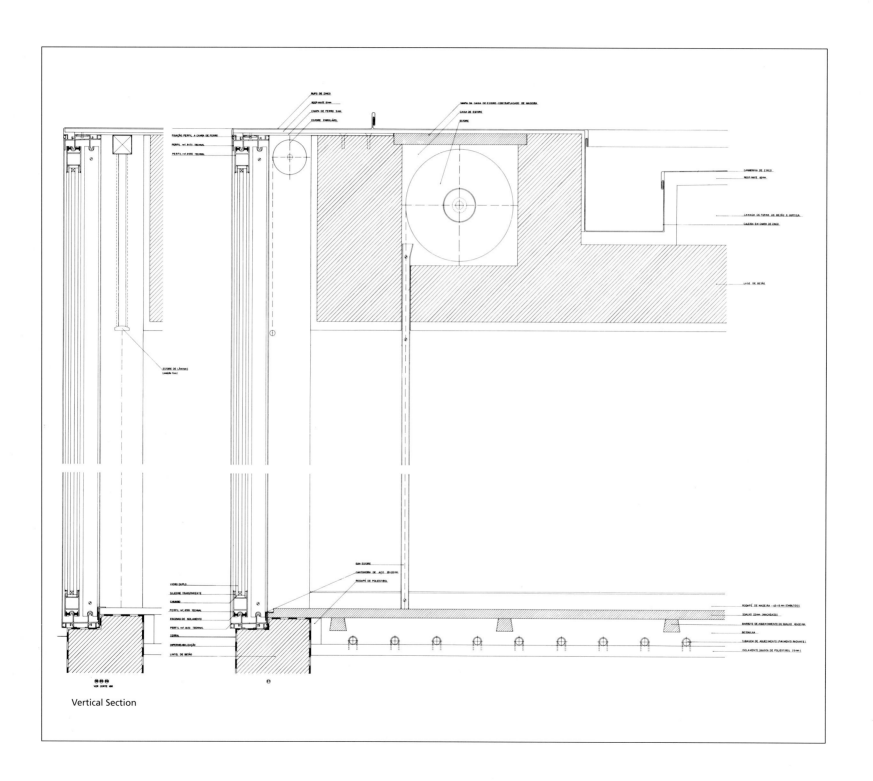

Vertical Section

Bom Jesus House

Braga, Portugal

One project consisting of two platforms, two stones, two programs, two construction systems, all forming two houses in one. The first level is for the children and consists of an "opus incertum," a stone box with doors and windows. The second level, for the parents, is a concrete box with a zinc roof and recessed floor-to-ceiling glass windows facing the balcony.

From the balcony, one sees the "market" and the appalling profile of Braga (the location of one of my first public projects, the municipal market).

Above: A water catchment takes on sculptural qualities, punctuating the terrain at the intersection of wall, path, and grass carpet.

Opposite Page: A rising, curved path gives way to this hilltop residence, whose contours and materials are reinforced by the granite wall comprising the first level of the two-story building.

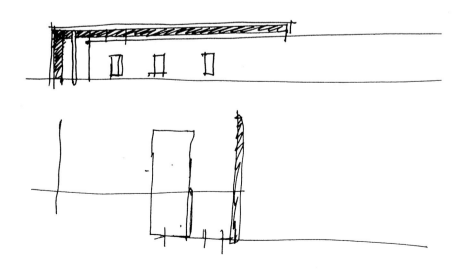

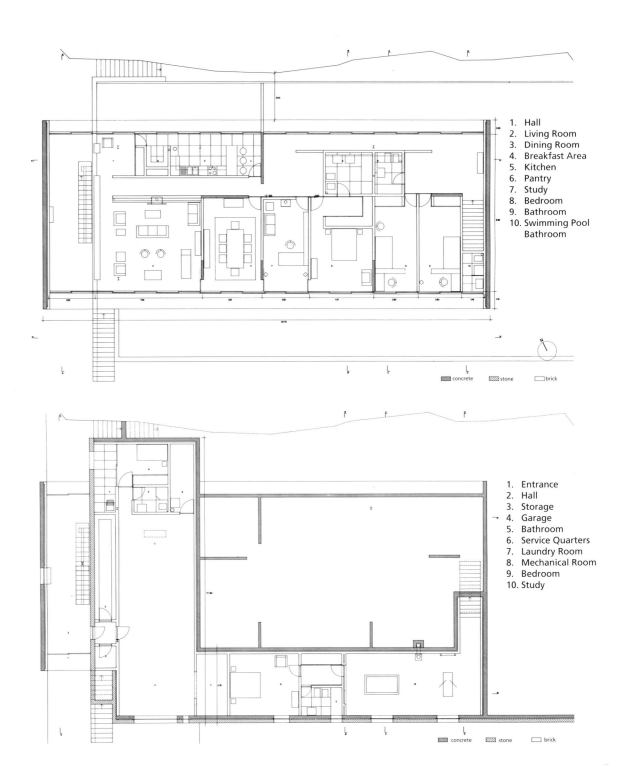

1. Hall
2. Living Room
3. Dining Room
4. Breakfast Area
5. Kitchen
6. Pantry
7. Study
8. Bedroom
9. Bathroom
10. Swimming Pool Bathroom

concrete   stone   brick

1. Entrance
2. Hall
3. Storage
4. Garage
5. Bathroom
6. Service Quarters
7. Laundry Room
8. Mechanical Room
9. Bedroom
10. Study

concrete   stone   brick

This Page: *Geometrically harmonic, an open swimming pool flanks the southeast elevation. A detail of the entry facade reveals the stair's incline as framed by a white and glass cover. From the northwest, only the stair and wall, with a small, low, centrally placed window, are evident.*

Opposite Page: *The stone elevation, opening onto the garage, gives access to service and storage areas. Planes of the facade and upper tier of the house, though contrasting in material composition, are linked by their geometries.*

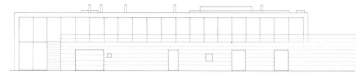

Southwest Elevation

Northwest Elevation

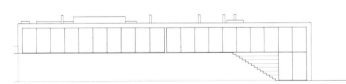

Northeast Elevation

Southeast Elevation

This Page: *Linear, wood-floored terraces, located at the front and back of the second floor, allow direct access to the outside through stone stairs.*

Opposite Page: *A curtain wall encloses a corridor along the northeast elevation, with bedrooms located behind. Adjacent to the swimming pool, it fronts onto a green, upwardly sloping terrain.*

This Page: *An interior stair connects the ground floor to the living room on the first floor. The iron railing and wood steps of the stair contrast with the solid volumes defined by the stone wall and terra-cotta floor.*

Opposite Page: *A linear skylight lets in shafts of light into the master bathroom. Some of the interior walls are mirrored to reflect the white plaster and grey marble used in the bathroom's construction.*

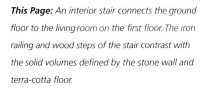

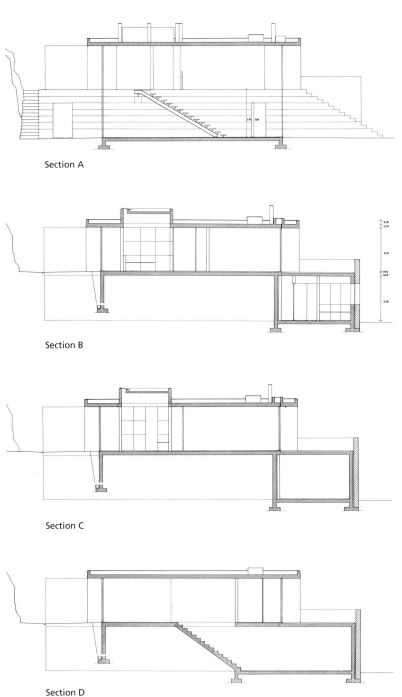

Section A

Section B

Section C

Section D

concrete   stone   brick

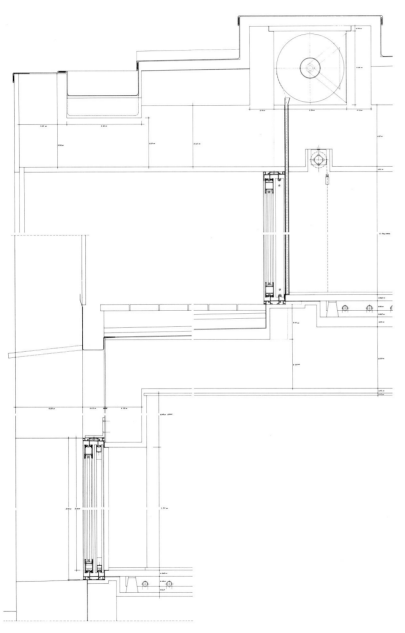

Vertical Section Through Southwest Facade

This Page: Details of the living room expose its various geometries and textures, evident in the interplay of windows, column, railing, and free-standing wood panels.

Opposite Page: View of the living room upon entering the second floor from the interior stair. Framed by a curtain wall and wood cabinets and walls, a metal girder punctuates the composition.

Baião House
Baião, Portugal

The client required a weekend house with limited dimensions to be built at the site of a ruin. The basic project was to restore the ruin as a walled garden and to build the house to one side. Work began with the demolition of the retaining wall and preparatory excavation—producing the house in its inverted image. The house itself is a concrete box surrounded by earth, but open toward the Douro River. The program required a "Portuguese house," one that is integrated into the landscape, or, in this case, almost buried in it.

It was still possible, even with a tight budget, to include Technal window frames from France, Sika fabrics from Switzerland, Dow Roofmate from the United States, Belgian roof gutters and drains made by the Compagnie Royale Asturienne des Mines, Rocca bathroom appliances from Spain, Italian fixtures from Mamoli, and Italian lamps.

Local materials ranged from pieces taken from a demolition site in Barredo, tiles from Leiria, and cabinet-making from Paredes provided by Mr. Reis, with whom I had worked earlier in Miramar. This text reminds me of a local song entitled "I Want to See Portugal in the E.C."

Above: *Ducts and vents in the roof push through the ceiling like the scattered stones that punctuate the grass above the site.*

Opposite Page: *With deep respect for the landscape, the residence was defined by an existing ruin and placed within its confines. A glass wall is the sole indication that the landscape has been altered in any way. The two coexist, the new structure blending seamlessly with the old.*

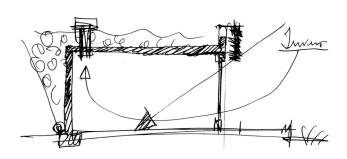

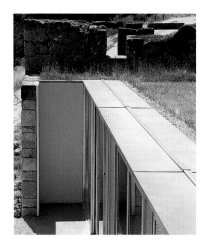

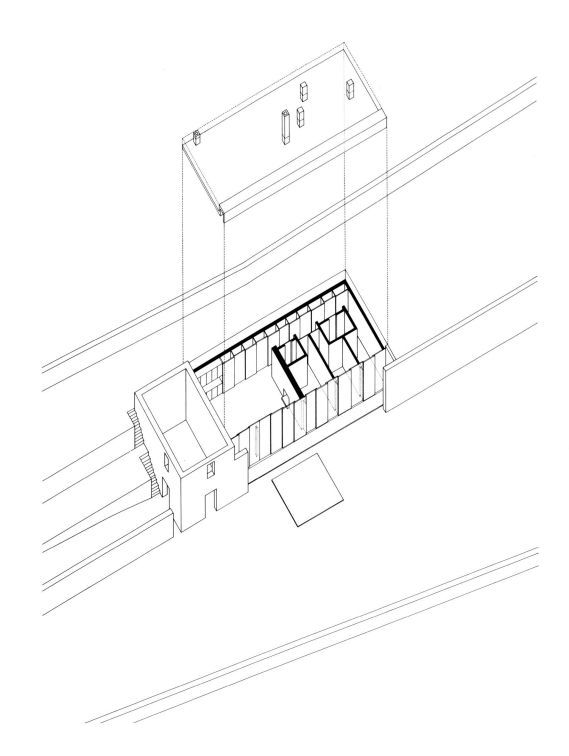

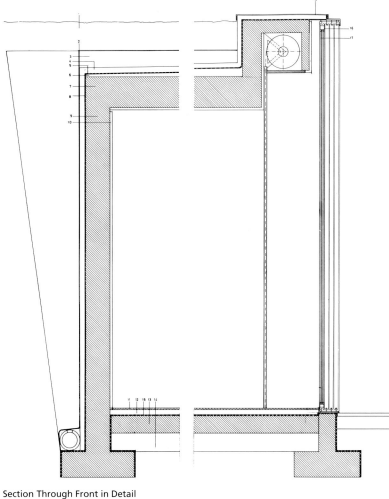

Section Through Front in Detail

1. Earth
2. Geotextile filter
3. Gravel
4. Thermal insulation
5. Steam barrier
6. Concrete
7. Lightened concrete
8. Steam barrier
9. Reinforced concrete
10. Plaster
11. Terra-cotta tiles
12. Concrete
13. Lightened concrete
14. Gravel
15. Galvanized protection board
16. Window frame
17. Double glazing
18. Waterproofing

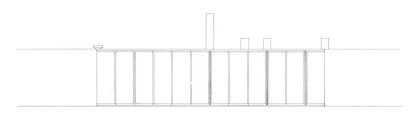

Main Elevation South 1/50

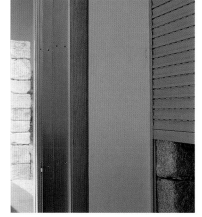

This Page: *Though condensed, a triple-rail system of windows allows the living space to be opened to the outdoors. Aluminum frames are inset between the wall and stone embankments.*

Opposite Page: *Wood-paneled storage areas, condensed along a single, narrow corridor, focus views to the outdoors. The warm colors of the wood contrast with the terra-cotta floors and the stone wall.*

Maia House
Maia, Portugal

N o excuses need be made for this house in Maia: despite the problems that come with every project, it turned out as I intended. There was no need to justify its form, typology, system of construction, or materials. This may seem strange but that's the way it was.

It so happens that for this project, I was both client and architect. A house should be designed by an architect for the architect. As an author assumes a pseudonym, an architect must assume an identity that adjusts to the client.

Only then can we respond to real needs such as shaving with the morning light, watching television with a fire burning in the fireplace, relaxing in the basement while the sun shines or the rain falls, or sleeping in the shade of a tree.

Analogical in program, orientation, and plot size, this house is based on the redesign of another house—the first one I ever built. The transmutation process was guided by ideas and discourse on inversion, collateral developments, and interconnections and omissions, in a path to muteness.

Architecture should be mute and opaque, but never deaf. This is probably the reason I was not asked to do the interior decoration.

Above: Windows facing the main road are veiled by trees that allow light while simultaneously keeping the bedrooms private.

Opposite Page: Compositional elements— walls, fenestration, and gate—are subtly linked to give character to the basic rectilinear volume. A textured palette is viewed from the entry, with metal, stone, painted stone, and plaster interacting.

This Page: *A private drive, bordered on one side by a wall and surrounding fields, encloses access to the main entrance, patios, garage, and garden. These patios, with mirrored, wall apertures, are connected to a line of trees in the front, to an opening that lets light and air into the basement, and to an open-air dining area that leads to the pool.*

Opposite Page: *The plan divides the residence into two rectilinear volumes, which are enclosed by stone walls.*

Right: *Situated by the main entry, narrow rectilinear planes of diverse texture are centered around the attenuated volume of an evergreen tree.*

Opposite Page: *Details of the entry reveal the confluence of foliage, stone, stucco, and a glass wall with steel frame and wood-screen paneling. Opening confronting hall doors gives an overview of interior and exterior spaces.*

Basement Plan
(left)

1. Laundry Room
2. Pantry
3. Patio
4. Storage
5. Kitchen

Ground-Floor Plan
(right)

1. Lot Entrance
2. House Entrance
3. Patio
4. Hall
5. Bathroom
6. Bedroom
7. Kitchen
8. Dining Room
9. Living Room
10. Swimming Pool
11. Garage

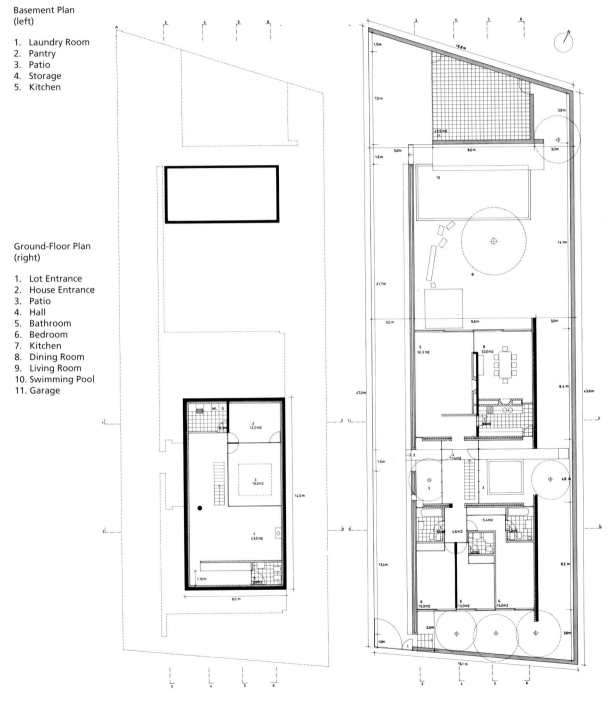

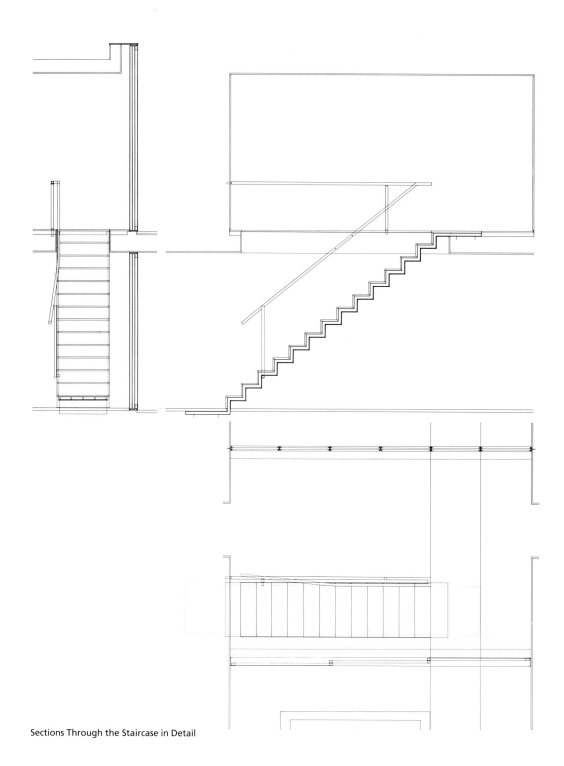

Sections Through the Staircase in Detail

This Page: *Composed of wood, the staircase echoes the surrounding floor pattern. Its stainless-steel railing reinforces the geometry of the window frames. A strip of marble visually connects opposite sides of the house.*

Opposite Page: *Interior views demarcate the tones, hues, and textures within the corridor leading to the living room. A staircase, located next to the second patio and facing the living room entry, leads to service and storage areas below.*

Right: The basement, housing the laundry room, pantry, storage, and a small kitchen is connected with the entrance hall by a pure and light wood staircase. A rectangular basement patio captures the light through a square, stucco opening.

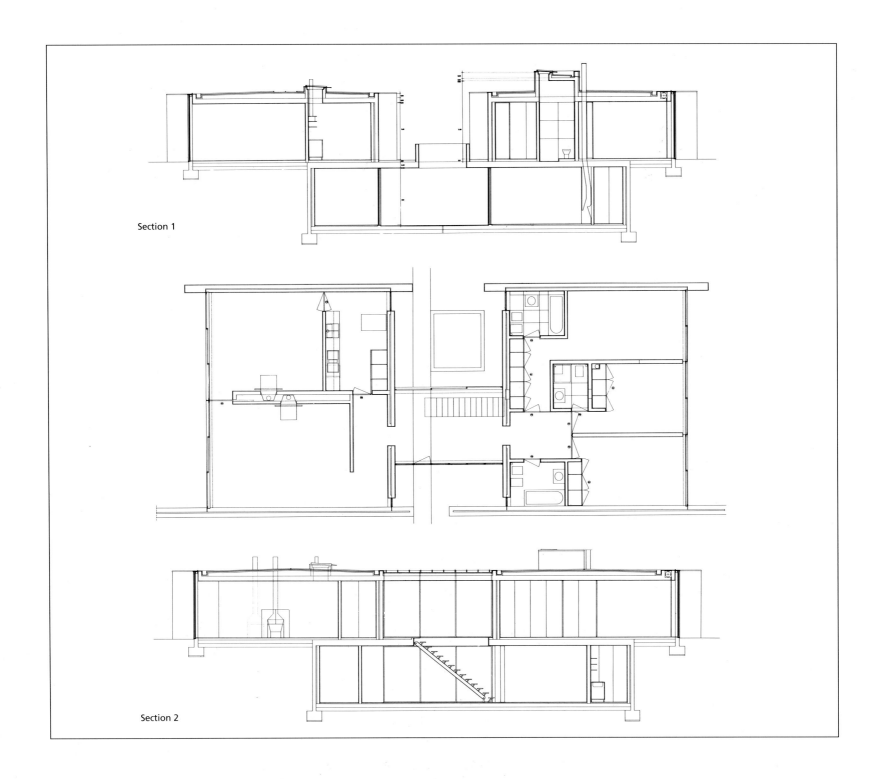

Section 1

Section 2

Tavira House

Algarve, Portugal

P ortugal is a place of synergies, where one plus one equals one. The south is really quite different. This house in Quinta do Lago was designed in Macao, while thinking of Le Corbusier's Chandigarh. Looking at a picture on a calendar of the Church of Light in Tavira, I noticed that there were many analogies between Le Corbusier and the Church.

There are no coincidences in this house on the Formosa tidal flats. The view of the churches in Tavira was planned before work began.

Above: *Viewed from the rear, the east elevation rises out of the landscape, its facade punctuated by three openings.*

Opposite Page: *The stark form of an orthogonal tower framed by rectilinear volumes rises along the crest of a hill. Its pure geometries contrast with the encircling forest, appearing far removed from any surrounding contexts.*

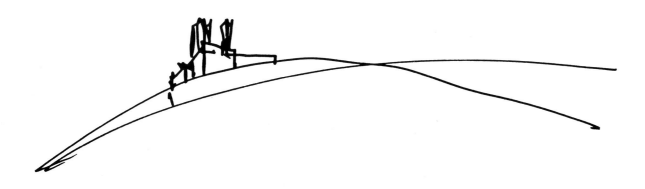

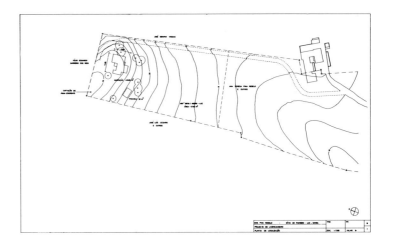

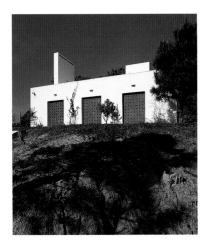

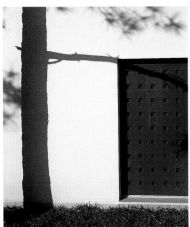

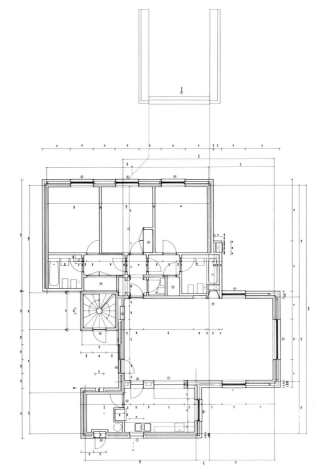

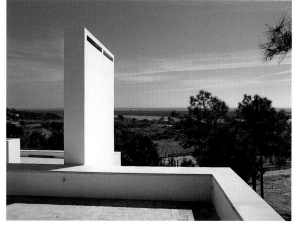

This Page: The southern facade opens the living room adjacent to the tower. A staircase situated on the northern edge of the residence provides roof access, where geometric planes and volumes abound against visually contrasting natural panoramas.

Opposite Page: The east elevation overlooking the hillside contains three bedrooms. Heavy gridded wood shutters reinforce the monastic feeling established by the austere lines of the house.

Right: *Sliding shutters open to reveal symmetrically aligned voids that cut through the living room in modular repetition.*

Opposite Page: *From the inside, openings frame the changing landscape. Dialogues between inside and outside, light and dark, stillness and movement, are established by the original resolution of the apertures.*

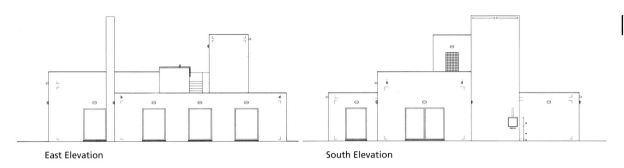

East Elevation   South Elevation

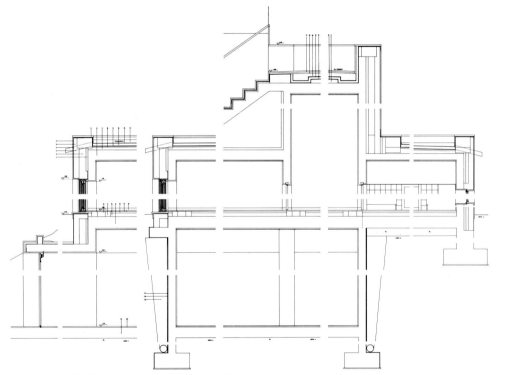

Composed Section Through the Facades, Root, and Interiors

West Elevation   North Elevation

Selected Buildings and Projects

Nevogilde House I

Rua do Padrão, Oporto, Portugal

Building size: 780 sf (237 m²)

Lot size: 2,150 sf (654 m²)

Date of Design: 1982

Construction Completion: 1985

Nevogilde House II

Rua de Nevogilde, Oporto, Portugal

Building size: 1,150 sf (350 m²)

Lot size: 9,850 sf (3,000 m²)

Date of Design: 1983

Construction Completion: 1988

Algarve House

Quinta do Lago Almansil,
Algarve, Portugal

Building size: 860 sf (262 m²)

Lot size: 5,250 sf (1,600 m²)

Date of Design: 1984

Construction Completion: 1989

Alcanena House

Casal dos Cardos, Zibreira,
Torres Novas, Portugal

Building size: 1,770 sf (540 m²)

Lot size: 164,000 sf (49,880 m²)

Date of Design: 1987

Construction Completion: 1992

Miramar House

Rua José Camarinha Barrote,
Vila Nova de Gaia, Portugal

Building size: 1,250 sf (380 m²)

Lot size: 11,800 sf (3,600 m²)

Date of Design: 1987

Construction Completion: 1991

Boavista Avenue House

Av. Boavista, Porto, Portugal

Building size: 1,750 sf (538 m²)

Lot size: 7,800 sf (2,388 m²)

Date of Design: 1987

Construction Completion: 1994

Bom Jesus House

Quinta da Batoca, Braga, Portugal

Building size: 1,380 sf (420 m²)

Lot size: 12,000 sf (3,670 m²)

Date of Design: 1989

Construction Completion: 1994

Baião House

Vale da Cerdeira, Baião, Portugal

Building size: 395 sf (120 m²)

Lot size: 69,000 sf (21,000 m²)

Date of Design: 1990–1991

Construction Completion: 1991–1993

Maia House

Nogueira-Maia, Portugal

Building size: 970 sf (296 m²)

Lot size: 2,400 sf (724 m²)

Date of Design: 1990–1991

Construction Completion: 1991–1993

Tavira House

Luz de Tavira,
Algarve, Portugal

Building size: 515 sf (157 m²)

Lot size: 18,700 sf (5,700 m²)

Date of Design: 1991

Construction Completion: 1994

Eduardo Souto Moura

1977–1997

Luísa Penha

João Mesquita

João Carreira

António Barbosa

Manuela Lara

Luís Barbosa da Silva

Daniel Oliveira

Paula Santos

Carlos Machado

António Lousa

José Fernando Gonçalves

Graça Correia

Francisco Vieira de Campos

Anne Wermeille

Luís Filipe Almeida d'Eça

Marie Clement

Teresa Gonçalves

Pedro Mendes

João Nuno Rodrigues Pereira

David Adjaye

Adriano Pimenta

Filipe Pinto da Cruz

Alvaro Leite

Francisco Cunha

Silvia Alves

Frederico Durão

Laura Peretti

Pedro Reis

José Carlos Mariano

Nuno Graça Moura

Camilo Bastos Rebelo

Joana Ribeiro

Manuela Carvalho

Tomás Neves

Lisandra Mendonça

Guilherme Machado Vaz

Oporto, Portugal, in 1952, Eduardo Souto de Moura graduated from the Oporto School of Architecture in 1980 where he later taught as an assistant professor until 1991. He has been a visiting professor at Harvard, Dublin, Zurich, and Lausanne.

In 1980, after working with Álvaro Siza since 1974, he established his own practice in Oporto and started designing a vast range of buildings, such as private houses and interior renovations, art galleries, a market in Braga, a cultural center in Oporto, a university building in Aveiro, a transport museum in Oporto, a residential block in Oporto, and the conversion of the Mosteiro de Santa Maria do Bouro into a state inn.

Other works by Moura include a project for the Ponte dell'Accademia in Venice (Biennale di Venezia), 1985; a hotel in Salzburg, 1987; a project for the Porta dei Colli, Palermo, Sicily (Triennale di Milano), 1987; the exhibition Um Museu Português Serralves in Expo'92 (Sevilha); and an installation at the Architektur Forum in Zurich.

Moura's work has been featured in numerous publications and exhibited in Portugal, France, Great Britain, Italy, Croatia, the United States, and Switzerland.

Moura has won several awards, including the first prize for the SEC cultural center in Oporto, 1981; the first prize for the redesign of Praça do Giraldo in Évora, 1982; the first prize in a competition for a hotel in Salzburg, 1987; the National Secil Award of Architecture, 1992; the International Prize for Stone in Architecture, 1995; and the Annual Award of the Portuguese Department of the International Association of Art Critics, 1996.

Photographic Credits